A PRACTICAL INTRODUCTION TO THE ART OF PREACHING

Edition 2020

Published by Mission All Nations Christian
Fellowship Ltd

ISBN -13-978-1-62407-767-8
ISBN -10- 1-62407-767-8

Second Edition 2020

Bible Quotes are from the New King James
Version or from the New International Version
unless otherwise started.

Table of Contents

Introduction 4

The historical background of The Art of Preaching 6

Why one has to preach? 16

The Preacher's Message Contents: 21

The Environment and Audience 31

Different Structures of a Sermon 41

Types of Sermons 47

The Mechanisms of Sermon Delivery 53

For Further reading: 57

The effects of postmodernity on today's evangelism

and their impact upon contemporary Christian faith, ...59

References: 74

INTRODUCTION

The purpose of this book is to explore summarily and step by step the main known ingredients of the Art of Preaching whether a preacher is compelled to preach indoor or at the open air meetings. It by no means covers every known method and principles of preaching but it does contain some tried and practical ideas that are sufficient to cover the practical introduction of the Art of Preaching at the academic standard level 1.

It should also be approached with a mindset that a 21st century Preacher is at the completion stage of God's long project of crushing Satan's head (Gen 3:15) and is dealing with a generation of people who "hears with its eyes and thinks with its feelings"[1]. In other words, the preacher is advised to take notice of the changing preaching environment and readjust the message or sermon as well as the delivery method accordingly. I still believe that these few lines will become a blessing to many.

May the Holy Spirit keeps revealing you the dynamic

---

1   Erwin W.Lutzer , Who are you Judge?,Learning to Distinguish between Truths, Halth-Truths and Lies, page 24

methodology to outreach everyone.
God bless you richly.

THE HISTORICAL BACKGROUND OF THE ART OF PREACHING

In his book, '*The Art of Preaching*', Charles Smyth, then canon of Derby, states: "I can conscientiously aver that in my own experience [...]I have hardly ever heard a really bad sermon, a sermon from which there was no instruction to be gained nor pleasure to be had. Yet it is clear that our sermons might be better than they are if the art of preaching were more studied.[1]"

Smyth also believes that "If the clergy are not taught how to preach, it is equally true that barristers are not taught how to plead [...]. The point is that the technique of preaching is something that can be taught, and therefore should be taught: and until it is taught, this reckless wastage of energy and of efficiency will continue."[2]

In fact the Art of Preaching can be traced as back as in the Old Testament times where prophets were referred to as preachers. Among them include Moses[3], who brought a direct message

---

1   Charles Smyth, The Art of Preaching, P. 15
2   Ibid., P. 15
3   "These are the sermons Moses preached to all Israel when they were east of the Jordan River..." Deuteronomy

from God to the Israelites, born in an environment of pluralistic gods, a message that has transformed them from their old ways of sympathising with belief in many gods to a belief in one and unique God.

Moses's sermons were then always referred to by many other prophets4 such as Isaiah (Isaiah 61:1), Ezekiel (Ezekiel 20:46), Jonah (Jonah 3:1), almost all post exilic prophets and as well as Jesus himself as delivered by a prophet or preacher.

Though the preaching ministry can be regarded as an art, it is also a prophetic ministry because it requires special characteristics and special connections with God, otherwise preaching without such special characteristics and God's connections may not achieve its intended aims.

It is because of those special characteristics that give credit to a preacher, the Young Jesus was given a platform by the Nazareth

---

1:1
4   Ezra 6:18; Nehemiah 3.1; Daniel 9:11–13; and Malachi 4:4

Synagogue's leaders with due respect when he made his initial entry into the Synagogue to announce his ministry's manifesto. One of the important declarations he ever made at his first public appearance was that he has been anointed:

"[1]to **preach** (**εναγγελίσασθαι**) the gospel to the poor, [2] to **proclaim** (**κηρύξαι**) liberty to the captives and [3 to] recovery of sight to the blind...[and 4] to **proclaim** (**κηρύξαι**) the acceptable year of the Lord[5]". In his speech, he specifically selected two words, *preach* and *proclaim* as his main tasks for his upcoming role. Commonly these two words (preach and proclaim) have been often used interchangeably, though in a context there could be small differences in nuances of meaning.

For instance Uprichard in his article [6]*"Preaching in New Testament'*, he states that [to]"preach or **Αγγελω- [Angello]** and its derivatives that includes **εναγγελίσασθαι** constitute the offer of information or encouragement in terms of its proclamation

---

[while] **κηρύξω - proclaim** tends to indicate a public and authoritative announcement which demands compliance[7]"

The English Dictionary states that 'preach' originated with the Latin word 'praedicare', to proclaim, and defines it as:

(1) to deliver a sermon or (2) to exhort. It also defines 'proclaim' as to make known by announcing in a public place or to publish abroad.

But 'preaching' is public speaking in which a 'preacher' lectures on a subject which might not even proclaim the gospel. A preacher's audience is not permitted to question him, dialogue during the preaching or even make a comment.

However the intention here is not the exegesis of these two words, but to just pick up some variations due to their contexts.

What is known in the New Testament times is that the most prominent preacher before Jesus was John Baptist. Even to this very day, no one can beat his controversial sermons where he could

---

7   Uprichard, R.E.H, *Preaching in the New Testament,* pages 2-3 (Dr. Uprichard is the Pastor of Trinity Presbyterian Church, Ahoghill in County Antrim, Northern Ireland)

easily compel his hearers to repent of their sins, despite calling them "sons of vipers" and yet those responding to his message were seen coming forward to be baptised into the Jordan River (Matthew 3:5-11). Jesus himself has acknowledged John the Baptist to be greater among all those born of women (Matthew 11:11). After John Baptist's era, the Apostles and many of the Early Church Fathers have followed suit of John Baptist and Jesus in preaching the Good News.

According to Clement of Rome (30-100), the Epistle to the Corinthians was itself a homily or a sermon.

This led Clement of Alexandria (160-220) to open up a Theological School in Alexandria to specifically instruct candidates for church membership in the principles of Christianity. He surely believed that preaching should be taught in a systematic way.

During the same period, Tertullian (150-230) who was a lawyer converted to Christianity at the age of
30 began to preach.

Nothing however is specified to whether Tertullian has attended Clement of Alexandria's Theological School.

As time went on, though the art of preaching was becoming so important in the first five centuries; it later began to decline in the early medieval period, between 430-1095, due presumably to many issues including the fact that the days of persecution were almost over.

It is common when the bad days are over, often seeking for godly things declines. In addition to this, it would not be surprising that often most of the sermon's themes are regularly linked with the situation of the time.

For instance at the time of writing these notes, it would not be surprising to hear most of the sermons' themes having connection with 'breakthroughs', 'joy comes in the morning' (Psalm 30:5), ' darkness over the land of Egypt and light in Goshen' (Exodus 10:22-23) and so on due to the current economic constraints connected with the western recession.

Though preaching themes may often vary due to the influence of seasons, preaching has been one the main tools to fulfil the Great Commission throughout the Church history. In the medieval period it began a new awakening of preaching where people like Saint Francis of Assisi (1182-1126), began a street preaching speaking the common language of ordinary people. He ended up to start the Franciscan order of monks having main themes of repentance and Gospel living. He was known to challenge his listeners to live simply and to focus on their relationship with Christ and service to their fellow men.

Other key figures during the medieval period were (1)John Wycliffe (1320-1384) who translated the Bible into the language of the people and (2) John Huss (1369-1415) who vigorously attacked the papacy and corruptions of the church through sermons and writings.

Several years later, during the reformation period, preaching was restored to the central place in worship and the Bible was underlined to be the only recognised source of supreme authority.

From the reformation period to the beginning of the English revival under Whitfield and Wesley rose other remarkable preachers including John Bunyan, a fervent preacher influenced by Luther, who was opposed by the Church of England for his preaching style, later jailed for 12 years and who was afterwards offered bail if he would stop preaching. Everyone was shocked by his response to the bail offer where he said: "If you let me out today I should preach tomorrow"[8].

Another known prominent British Evangelist of that time who was converted upon reading Luther's preface to Romans is John Wesley (1703-1791); he preached all over England more than any before him and is credited to be the founder of the Methodist movement.

After him came Charles Spurgeon (1834-1892), a great preacher with sense of humor who left behind 38 volumes of his sermons which are available even today.

The history of Art of Preaching would not be complete without mentioning D.L. Moody (1837-1899) who believed in inerrancy

8   Christiana's Progress part II, Adapted From, Orion's Gate's page 2

of the Scriptures and a great persuasive and powerful evangelist of his time.

Besides all the heroes of faith in the domain of preaching one may also include Billy Graham who is almost the world's most famous preacher and the most effective evangelist of the post-war period.

Although much has been written about his life, his contribution to the unity of the church, global and local, yet little is known about him at least in Britain on his methods of sermon preparation or delivery in the area of Art of Preaching. At the time of these notes, Billy Graham is 93 and is still an icon to the world's evangelism.

In addition to the above long list of the heroes in the area of preaching, one may also include Renhard Bonke, a powerful German born preacher and Evangelist to the African continent, who has an ambitious programme to empty hell and populate heaven and who sees Africa to being saved shortly. According to his statistics, in 2002 'Christ for all Nations', Bonke's evangelistic preaching organisation, wanted to win 10 to 12 million people for Christ, and in the first ten years of the 21st century the overall aim was to win a total of 100 million people.

If you are today a trainee or experienced preacher, you are not alone but surrounded by a crowd of heroes of faith in the domain of preaching.

WHY ONE HAS TO PREACH?

One of the main texts that gives New Testament's preachers a mandate to preach is the great commission as it is said in Mark 16:15,16: "Go ye into all the world, and **preach the gospel** to every creature. He that believeth and is baptized shall be saved; but he that believeth not shall be damned".

I would like to emphasis that in translating the command "go" does not make a preaching's pre-requisite a move from point A to B., for it would invalidate the Acts 1:8 mandate where the disciples' initial starting point was to be Jerusalem, where they were already.

What can only be drawn from the Great Commission is that Preaching is a Biblical mandate from Jesus himself as well as from many other Biblical references.

For instance in (1)1 Corinthians 1:17-18 -17 it is said " **Christ did** not **send me** to baptize, but **to preach the gospel**", in (2) 2 Timothy 2:2, Paul urges Timothy saying " the things that you have heard from me among many witnesses, **commit these to faithful men who will be able to teach others"** also

(3) in Proverbs 9:9 the writer states **"give instruction** to a wise man, and he will be still wiser; **teach** a just man, and he will increase in learning", in other words, instructing God's people is not an option but a mandate.

It is also to be remembered that preaching and teaching are often interconnected because, as said earlier, to proclaim (from the Greek word **κηρύσσω** -keruso) may have root in Kerygma which were the early apostles' teaching.

Finally in (4) 1 Corinthians 1:23-24 Paul feels compel to " **preach** Christ crucified",

However all the above Biblical references do not give a straight line or one off definition of what should be the meaning preaching.

In a day to day language, preaching requires speaking, opening a mouth; in some other situations however, such as in 1 Cor 11:26, Paul suggests that even eating bread or partaking the

Holy Communion or Lord's Supper is also an act of declaration or publication (Katangelo - καταγγέλλω) a way of announcing to the public about the Lord's death.

It infers then that preaching is not an isolated act because preaching is the whole series of dynamic interactions between the preacher, the Scriptures, the present time and situation.

A plain reading of certain texts may have its own impact on the minds and hearts of the listeners, but many other passages are not so immediately accessible.

Preaching seeks to do today, for the current congregation, what the passage did for the original listeners/readers. Such dynamism of the Scriptures is a part of modern Applied theology.

So preaching is more than just attempting to discover the author's original intent. It accepts that Scripture not only *says* certain things but also *does* certain things.

A preacher does not only an attempt to discover what Scripture says to people on a particular day but seeks also to discover what God wants to do for, with and through this particular congregation.

Preaching takes place when a number of factors intersect in time and space. Four main factors may be: (i) **the message**, (ii) **the preacher**, (iii) **the audience** and (iv) **the presence of God**.

Other factors may have an impact on sermon preparation, its delivery and outcome, but without these four basic ones, "preaching" will not be having its full essence.

In all of this, when a preacher stands in presence of a congregation is to declare the Word of God and not to show off some of the Christian theologies or principles of Christian morality.

Some of the young theologians (or Preachers) fall often into a trap of quoting some Greek words as a sign of authority.

Though there is nothing wrong by backing one's message with some Greek or Hebrew, but dwelling upon them may be regarded, to some extend, by the audience as a way of showing off higher knowledge of the Scriptures, and it is advisable to avoid such practice.

The basic core of preaching is to expose the Biblical truth to People. It is not merely presenting them ex cathedra, but living out a life of faith in Christ among those same people even once the sermon is over.

The preacher's whole lifestyle is meant to be dedicated to being a presentation of the Gospel. This can't be done by just few words in a sermon on Sunday or weekday service.

That is how there is no straight definition that can be found to explain what may constitute a best sermon, because sermons are part of the preacher's day to day lifestyle in the community.

THE PREACHER'S MESSAGE CONTENTS:

As Preaching is not only done because someone has a preaching call or is an excellent public speaker, there are a number of good ingredients of a Biblical based sermon to meet the basic required standards.

A standard sermon then should include among others (a) **A Theme** and an appropriate **Text**, (b) a **Statement**, (c) some **illustrations** to make a sermon be understood, (d) **eventually Supportive Testimony** and (e) a short **Conclusion** as a sum up.

Every good sermon must be based on Scriptures and not on mere baseless stories. If a preacher is to speak with authority,he/she must use every opportunity to quote, teach, and honour the Scriptures (2 Tim 4:1-5).

Sermons that are not structured are often endless.

(a) A theme and appropriate text:

A theme is almost a summary of the entire sermon. If one asks you to preach one minute, you can just sum up your sermon in its theme and the whole message may be understood.

If the theme is chosen first, then the text must support the theme without distorting or accommodating the text.

Suppose one is going to preach on the Great Commission, Matt 28:18-20.

It can approached from different angles having theme "The Great Commission ,an Unfinished Commission".

The sermon may be divided into 4 parts:

1. The Mission

2. Evangelising

3. Baptising and Church Planting

4. Teach disciples - Consolidation

Young preachers are often bullied by experienced ones to abandon the traditional organisational way of sermons where a theme is divided into different points.

Commonly there is nothing wrong to divide a sermon into different points as it guides a preacher to remain within the framework of the text.

Those who walk away from the conventional sermon preparation often preach an endless sermon because of poor planning.

A. Select Text

In the same method of planing for a sermon, a text is framed into a statement as it was intented by the author. In choising the statement, a preacher is advised to avoid the use of single words because a theme should be, as said earlier, almost a summary in one sentence of the entire sermon. A statement should be read within the general framework of the context. Texts or context that accommodate an application that is foreign to the original author's intend or the general ethics of the Scriptures should be avoided.

For instance the verse, "Let us do evil that good may come" is from Romans 3:8, but when it is removed from its general context, it may contradict the entire teaching of the Scriptures.

There is no where the Bible can contract its general cohesion and ethics.

Furthermore,no text gets genuinity or authenticity for just being quoted by numerous famous preachers.

On other hands, there should not be any fear of using common text that has been used by most of the great preachers just for being thought of being a novice in the area of preaching. This however does not say that a preacher should copy people's sermons because a message always speaks uniquely to a given audience.

When choosing a main text to preach on, it is sometimes recommended to avoid texts or portions of the Scriptures which were added from marginal notes, and not found in the oldest and most reliable manuscripts.

Also avoid to introduce the message by quoting the author of the book you are not sure of. For instance if the text is chosen from

Hebrews, it is not advisable to say 'my message today is from **the Epistle of Paul to Hebrews**'.

That is a common mistake among young preachers where they think of all New Testament Epistles are from Paul. The wrong authorship and marginal notes may be sometimes misleading. You would even be surprised to hear one reading from **the book of the prophet Nehemiah**; such book does not exist.

The texts taken from the marginal notes or from the no reliable manuscripts do not mean that they necessarily contain false teaching, but a sermon based on a contested text or wrong quotation may not gain authority with such people who know of them.

In the same line, Preachers should avoid choosing text from the Apocrypha writings or other uninspired sayings though being inserted into the Bible, they may not have Divine authority. Some of them for instance are those addressed by Job's friends in the Book of Job. One may also get some sayings included into the Scriptures such as those quote from the Devil in Luke 4, the words of Pharaoh, Balaam, Pilate, and other men whose words are reported, but who are not inspired Apostles or Prophets.

It would not be surprising to meet someone from the catholic background saying from time to times "the Holy Scriptures say that a just man sins seven times a day".

Though this saying has become common, it is written nowhere in the Bible.

That is why, it is recommended, as aforesaid, for a preacher to avoid such odd or strange texts that even found in the Scriptures.

Before a text can be expressed in an intelligent theme, it must be properly interpreted.

The following guidelines could be useful for interpreting the Scriptures:

1. Keep the text in its context.

Scripture, which seems to have one meaning may actually mean something quite different when read in their original context.

For instance I Corinthians 2:9 quoting Isaiah 64:4 seems to refer to the heaven's future glory, yet the context reveals it to be a quotation from the Old Testament predicting fuller revelations of the dispensation of grace, which we may enjoy in this present world.

Colossians 2:21 says to "...touch not, taste not, and handle not...," and appears to be a good prohibition text and often used in some conservatives "milieu" to back up text to stamp up the old principles which they would like to keep such as in the use of alcohol. However there are other good texts against beverage alcohol in the Scriptures more than using Colossians 2:21.

(c) Illustration

A sermon is better understood if it is framed into a short statement and supported by illustrations. Illustrations are often viewed as windows of a sermon in the similar way windows are for a house. A sermon without illustrations is often hard to grasp and may even be boring.

(d) Supporting Testimonies:

That is why it is an added value to a sermon, if it includes testimonies when it is possible to bring the truth of what you to say live to an audience.

It is also to be remembered to apply the text with today's context and audience.

(e) Conclusion:

Finally at the end of every sermon it is recommended to sum it up before capping it up with a conclusion. When you come to the end of a sermon, do not forget to go over the sermon's main points starting from its introduction.

In so doing it is like wrapping up the whole package together like a bouquet of flowers which makes the sermon much clearer to the audience.

Length of a sermon

Some of the Charismatic preachers think that preaching too long make the message more clearer. One of the most challenging parts of the sermon's preparation and delivery, mainly in the charismatic context, is its length. The audience finds it hard to follow an extreme long sermon to the degree that some may even fall asleep.

Those long sermons are delivered in Paul's pattern (Acts 20:9) where a young man fell down on the balcony during Paul's sermon. Avoid then such similar incidents where a preacher would be obliged to restart a new ministry of resurrecting people from dead due to his excessive endless sermon.

In some youth oriented audience, one would be surprised to hear an incessant "amen" from the audience as they are being edified by the message.

However if a preacher is hearing too many "amen", he should double check to whether they are pleased with the message or if it is a polite way of shutting him up.

30

A sermon should not be longer than one hour for special occasions, such as a Gospel or Revival meeting.

But commonly Sunday's service sermon should be between 30-45 minutes long. A sermon powerfully preached in half an hour is better than one dragged on and on for an extra 15 minutes.

THE ENVIRONMENT AND AUDIENCE

A preacher may preach in the open air meeting as well as in the building. Depending on the audience, a modern preacher takes into consideration the environment before preaching to the public. The New Testament speaks of one occasion when Jesus entered into one of the boats, to preach the multitude from the boat (Luke 5:3).

This method of preaching may be considered by modern day preachers as having taken into consideration, audience and environment by using right tools and speaking clearly to the audience. He probably decided to preach from the boat for two reasons: (1)to avoid the crowd pushups and (2) to face the entire audience. It could even be for holistic reason because water can sometimes serve as resonance tool to amplify the voice.

In whichever way, he did consider his audience and environment.

(a) Outside (Open air) preaching

The background of outside (or open air) preaching may be traced back to the Old Testament time where they had limited tools of communication and their style of communicating the word was often done at the gates by the prophets.

For instance in **(1) Judges 9:7** it is said that "Jotham **went and stood in the top of Mount** Gerizim, and lifted up his voice, and **cried**, and said unto them, Hearken unto me, ye men of Shechem, that God may hearken unto you."

Similarly in **(2) Jeremiah 7:1-2**: it is said that "The word that came to Jeremiah from the Lord, saying, Stand in the **gate** of the Lord's house, **and proclaim** there this word, and say, Hear the word of the Lord, all ye of Judah, that enter in at these gates to worship the Lord.

As it is in **(3) Jeremiah 17:19-20** where it is said "Thus said the Lord unto me, Go and stand in the **gate** of the children of the people, whereby the kings of Judah come in, and by the which they go out, and in all the **gates** of Jerusalem; and say unto them, Hear ye the word of the Lord, ye kings of Judah, and all Judah, and all the inhabitants of Jerusalem that enter in by these gates: Thus saith the Lord…"

And in **(4) Jeremiah 36:10** it is also said "Then read Baruch in the book of the words of Jeremiah in the house of the Lord… **at the entry of the new gate** of the Lord's house, in the ears of all the people."

Literally, it looks that the gateway call was one of the common ways to convey the message to a large audience.

The early New Testament preachers, such as John Baptist, Jesus and the Apostles have used almost similar method.

However Jesus was combining different methodologies such as one to one meeting, indoor communication and open air meeting. One may wonder whether if Jesus was still on earth would use a microphone and other modern medium technologies to communicate the message efficiently.

Open air communication has its own challenge that may be a hindrance to effective communication.

There would be no need to speak if no one is hearing.

As the infant church took its first steps into pagan culture, preaching was occurring largely outdoors. Nowadays the church preaching is becoming mainly indoors and in the context of the worship service. They could be other people who still believe that if a church needs to be an outreaching it should consider proper preaching to be done outside.

In such mood of disagreement, one may wonder to whether Church buildings should remain in place, in our current time, as they were designed to be if they do no longer serve the same purpose that of accommodating church services.

In whichever way, in case a preaching happens to be done in the open air, a preacher should take into consideration the environment, to whether it is too hot, or too cold, too noisy and so on. If it is too hot or cold, the message should be reasonable to avoid people leaving the stage before the preacher. It could be an embarrassing situation if a preacher is left by himself towards the end of the sermon while the whole audience has left before finishing the service.

Furthermore, preaching tools should be tested before the preacher starts to use them, otherwise, people may not follow the message and the whole effort may be wasted if the target aim is not achieved.

(b) Indoor preaching

In the similar way, indoor preaching may take place into buildings other than churches and chapels. In time of Spurgeon, preaching was used to take place even in barns, workhouses and even in music hall. Nowadays, the spoken word reaches people in their sitting room comfort through radio and television.

Often indoor preacher does not care much about the environment. However, though being in a comfort place, it may be overcrowded, hot, dark or even cold. All of these changes should not be ignored by the preacher.

If for instance the environment is hot, it would lead the audience to get sleepy. It is then the role of the preacher to avoid the Eutychus' incident stated above (Acts 20:6-12).

Another consideration would be to care about the young church or children present in the audience who would be bored if the voice remains monotone or message remains abstract. It is then as seen in other sessions to include some of the interactive material into the sermon such visual aids or illustrations.

Some of the practices to avoid during the preaching sessions:

Whether one is preaching in open air or indoor, it is recommended to:

(1)Turn off a mobile phone completely, as any vibration or ring tone may distract a preacher or the audience from the flow of the message.

(2) Take hands away from the mouth or pockets and speak clearly with confidence. For some people in the audience may be looking at the unwanted gesticulates such as crossed arms, and hands into a pocket or behind your back and this may distract the audience from hearing the message.

It is also often recommended to do not hammering the pulpit or make excessive move during the sermon delivery because it may disturb the attention of the audience or the recording if there is any. Even some of the elderly people may find hard to follow a highly moving preacher.

(3) Face the audience:

A preacher who looks down the entire time of the message may look as if he/she does not care about the audience or is not sure of what he/she is preaching about. It is good to make eye contact with the audience during the sermon delivery. However, it is good to focus on individuals in different areas and looking at them directly in the eyes for five to ten seconds because if one focusses on one area and too long, they may think that a preacher is picking on them.

(4) Maintain a steady voice at the beginning and at the end of each sentence so that the voice can be heard clearly at the conclusion of each thought.

(5) Mainly in the open air meeting, stay on schedule; If one is given ten minutes to speak. Make sure to leave the audience wanting more, not less. Be sure to practice the speech in advance within the specified time given. On speech day, ensure the watch is on top of or next to the podium to keep track of the time. Avoid what has become common to say this is an 'African time'.

(6) Remember, preaching like other public speaking is a learned skill that develops over time with patience. Young preachers are advised to practice the message with friends and family members and ask some feedbacks. Their main initial pulpit is their bathroom. Try it over and over before appearing to the public and remain cool and confident about what you do.

(7) If one has time, try even videotape or tape record the message, if necessary, to evaluate your delivery, articulation, and speed of speaking before appearing into the public arena.

Audience

The audience may be made by elderly, children, new converts even visitors, people from different backgrounds mainly in western society.

A preacher should take into consideration various groups that are in the audience.

Feedback of the message:

Every message should have a certain aim to achieve. Though a preacher is not bound to tell the audience of what he/she intend to achieve, all points should learn towards achieving the intended goal.

By the end of sermon, a preacher should expect a certain response that he/she should evaluate to whether the message has been understood at least by a large number of the congregation.

There are several ways of getting a feedback about the sermon preached.

In some churches, the audience has access to their preacher as they greet them at the door. Some members of the congregation come often to the preacher telling him/her nice sermon and so on. They may be other occasions where a preacher has a team of people who may inform him/her what to correct, if there is any. Those who are more formal use formal feedback.

This however is not required. In overall, whether indoor or outdoor preaching, the aim is to (1) transmit clearly the message to a given audience, this requires to set up some sort of feedback by which the audience responds to what they heard from the preacher for verification; (2) the preacher has also to ensure that the audience genuinely understands what is being said.

That is why commonly speaking, one should ensure that the one sitting at the far end listens clearly.

DIFFERENT STRUCTURES OF A SERMON

A preacher hears a message from God and puts it into a sermon structure to finally deliver it to the congregation.

In order to preach a message, however, one requires to understand the Biblical text, the audience and the context or environment.

A sermon may be made by a single verse, a pericope or on by several passages structured and central formulated on a given theme.

Most of the sermons have three main parts that are (1) an introduction, (2) a main body and (3) a conclusion at the end

The body of a sermon is the main preaching part and should be expanded to what is called outlines.

Some preachers prefer to start with a conclusion, followed by the sermon outlines and ending up with an introduction.

This is not however a normal way of structuring a sermon, it is only given for practical purposes.

As said, the sermon's outlines is your road map for writing sermons; it also help a preacher to remain focussed and to give the audience the direction where he/she heading to.

That is why when the sermon is well structured; the audience is able to follow it well.

Practically, this is one of the ways one may prepare a sermon:

Choose your text

Catch up some dominant thoughts in one short, clear, vivid sentence that would serve as a theme.

Read, re-read, and re-re-read the text to make sure you understand what it means. It often recommended to do not go for third party interpretation before you have formulated specific interpretive questions which you have been unable to answer, or until you have completed your interpretive work;

Develop appropriate outlines.

Carefully choose words that are precise, simple, clear, vivid and honest. Write out the key sections, phrases, and sentences to help you in your word choice. Stick to short declarative and interrogative sentences with few, if any, subordinate clauses.

Try to apply to your audience and come up with illustrations and examples.

Avoid making illustrations and examples so prominent that they detract from the dominant thought. Also, avoid applying them inappropriately or overusing them.

Add the introduction and conclusion.

The introduction should not be elaborate, but enough to arouse their curiosity, wet their appetites and introduce the dominant thought. This can be done by a variety of means: explaining the setting of the passage, story, current event or issue, etc.

The conclusion should not merely recapitulate your sermon but you should keep something for the end which will prevail upon your people to take action.

Sample of a sermon:

Text: Philippians 3:10,11.

Title: Knowing the power of Jesus' resurrection.

1. Introduction:

I want to know Christ and the power of his resurrection and the fellowship of sharing in his sufferings, becoming like him in his death.

2. I want to know him:

•What does "knowing Christ" mean?

•Jesus wants his followers to know him better (John 17:3).

•His divine power has given us everything we need through our knowledge of him. (2 Peter 1:3)

•If then Christ is not raised from the dead, his bones are still buried somewhere in Palestine, then we cannot know him

•Illustration: I know some of the books of Dr. William Kay who was used to teach at Mattersey Hall but I don't know him. To know him, I would have met him or maybe share with him a cup of tea.

•In the same way to know Jesus is not only to read about him, but to fellowship with him and if he is dead, there is nowhere you can fellowship with someone already dead.

3. I want to know the power of his resurrection:

•If he is not raised from the dead, then he has no power today, a dead man does not have any power

•We are justified because of the Power of his resurrection (Rom 4:25):

4. Share his sufferings:

•Christianity is a relationship with a living Saviour, a Saviour we can know, a Saviour who infuses our life and empowers us, who transforms us into his likeness

5. Conclusion:

•Do you truly believe that Jesus rose from the dead? Remember that if a man is dead, we might be reading about him but we cannot know him. Have you been able to know Jesus?

•Look what Paul wanted: (1) to know Jesus, and the power of his resurrection.

What do you really want more than anything else?

•Do you know the power of the resurrection in your life?

•If so Amen!

TYPES OF SERMONS

In a classical structure of sermons that are:

(1) Textual sermon:

A textual sermon is one based on short portion of Scriptures whether a single verse, a pericope or a whole book. For instance one may chose a text such as "Now is our salvation nearer than when we believed" (Rom 13:11) and investigate it and analyze it fully to discover all the truth it may contain to finally present it in an orderly manner to the congregation.

In some instances, a textual sermon may be divided into two parts that are (i) homily - homiletic sermon and (ii) thematic sermon

(i) A homily - Homiletic sermon is often presented in a dialogue form in which the audience poses questions and makes comments on the topic. Though this type of sermon is not common, it is more or less a Bible study style where people may discuss during the message delivery.

(ii) A thematic sermon is mainly argumentative. The principal thought of the text is condensed to a theme. The introductory

48

portion is an introduction to this theme, and the parts or divisions that follow are a logical, argumentative proof and development of the theme.

A textual - thematic sermon may be constructed around a sound based doctrine such (1) Soteriology - salvation; (2) Pneumatology - Holy Spirit; (3) Christology - Jesus Christ; (4) Eschatology - end time events; (5) Bibliology - the Bible; (6) Angelology - Angels, Satan, demons; (7) Anthropology - man; (8) The Virgin Birth; (9) The Blood Atonement; (10) Bodily Resurrection etc...

In a textual sermon, the preacher may use a particular text to make a point without examining the original intent of that text, this does not however say that a preacher preaches out of context.

(2) Topical sermon:

A topical sermon may be constructed around a topic such as (1) How to have a happy marriage - family; (2) Heaven and Hell (Luke 16); (3) How to have revival like our last Leicester East

Preacher's gesture and body language

In a church context, the congregation is expected a preacher to deliver a sermon with confidence. That is why a pastor is expected to stand with good posture, make good eye contact, and patiently deliver God's word.

The word is exciting if the body language send similar message or signals to the congregation.

Some sermons may send different signals to their hearers. For instance if someone is talking about hell with a smile in the face, or news about heaven with sad face, and so on, the message returns to the sender.

Whether a preacher is aware of it or not, a body language always send messages that often a preacher may not even be aware of such as anger or nervousness.

Before preaching, a preacher, mainly trainee preachers are advised to work on the following area of nonverbal communication including (1) Body, (2) Posture, (3) Eye contact, (4) Facial expression, (5)

Convention; (4) Effective outreaching in the City; (5) How to be a friend of God etc...

(3) Biographical sermon:

A Biographical sermon is the easiest sermon type as is always based on the study of the life of some great Biblical personalities such as (1) Abraham, the father who did not restrain his only son, (2) The wife of Lot, the backslidden; (3) Samson (4) Daniel, (5) Peter, James, etc...

(4) Allegorical sermon:

Allegory is a representation of abstract ideas or principles by characters, figures, or events in narrative, dramatic, or pictorial form. In regard to the Scriptures, there are some portions of the Bible that are written in a way they reveal not literal meaning but spiritual truth. One straight example of Biblical allegory can be read from Galates 4:22-31, where it is said that "Abraham had two sons, one by the slave woman and the other by the free woman. His son by the slave woman was born according to the flesh, but his son by the free woman was born as the result of a divine promise.

Which things are an allegory: for these are the two covenants; One covenant is from Mount Sinai and bears children who are to be slaves: This is Hagar.

Hagar stands for Mount Sinai in Arabia and corresponds to the present city of Jerusalem, because she is in slavery with her children".

Though some of the portions of the Scriptures are written in the allegorical way, a preacher is always advised, as said earlier, to remain in the context of the general ethics of the Scriptures if he/she choses to preach on such portion of the Scriptures.

(5)Expository sermon

The last part that is common in most of the sermons is the expository sermon.

An expository sermon may involve the exposition, or comprehensive explanation of the Scripture; presenting the meaning and intent of a Biblical text, providing commentary and examples and illustrations to make the passage clear and understandable. The goal is to expose the meaning of the Bible, verse by verse.

(6) Sermon based specific occasions:

Besides the above categories of sermons, it exists other type of sermons based on specific occasions such as (1) Wedding, (2) funerals, (3) Dedication of Children; (4) Father's day, (5) New year's; (6) Easter - Resurrection Day; (7) Christmas day; (8) Remembrance day etc...

Workshop:

Prepare 30 minutes sermon based on Matthew 8:9 "For I myself am a man under authority" to deliver into your Church taking into consideration the main part of the sermon including sermon structure, sermon contents and the delivery procedures.

THE MECHANISMS OF SERMON DELIVERY

Voice management

A preacher main aim is to make his message heard and one of the best ways to do so is to speak up in a reasonable and measurable tune to the degree those seating at the back end listen to the message. Speaking to those at the far end does not necessary mean shouting loud.

It is often difficult to draw a sharp line between the form of a sermon and its contents, between style and substance, between the medium and the message. What is true is that the aim of preaching is to enable people better listening to the gospel. For that reason, the preacher's main objective is to get his/ her audience getting much out of the message.

Arms and hands, (6) Body movement, (7) Tone, (8) voice's volume and so on.

Organised notes and note dependent

As we have just said, a preacher is advised to keep audience eye contact. The best way to do so is not to be dependent on the notes. Notes should be used to guide specific points, for quotations, and as an occasional help. Excessive use of notes distracts the congregation.

Always, as I said earlier, trainee preachers, are recommended to read through the notes sometimes aloud 3-4 times before delivery, make some reheasal and memorise, if possible the illustrations including where transitions are place and master the first three sentences and the last three of your sermon.

Illustrations and visual aids:

Use if possible illustrations from the surrendings. During his sermons, Jesus was taking illustrations from his surrendings. For instances in some occasions he was mentioning Lillies of the field, to make his message heard by the intended audience.

In modern days, people are attracked by technology and often use PowerPoint presentation. However in some environment, this technology may be of help but in some other places, it may distract hearers from following clearly the message mainly when it is mixed with too many images.

Appropriate conclusion in due time

As said in previous session, a preacher is reminded to cap up the sermon with appropriate conclusion and in due time.

Once again avoid Paul's style of sermon (Acts 20:9) where a young man fell down the window when paul was preaching.

Often a preacher who does not have preparation, may not know the right time to conclude the sermon. If he/she does not have prepared notes, he /she may not realise how long the sermon has lasted and may start to find it out when people begin to leave the stage one by one or start to pray for extra anoiting to endure the lengthy sermon. If a preacher is then not well prepared, he may decide to rush off to finish the message without approriate smoth transition.

Such rush would look like a flying plan that would soudainly make emergency landing which obviously would scare everyone on board.

In the same analogy, a preacher that finish a sermon without summing it up is like the craching pilot who would smash the plaine at the tarmac or runway.

Workshop

To finish the 30 minutes sermon based on Matthew 8:9 "For I myself am a man under authority" to deliver in Your Church.

FOR FURTHER READING:

Haddon W. Robinson, *Biblical preaching: The development and delivery of Expository messages*, Baker Book house, USA, 2001

Kenton C. Anderson, *Choosing to preach: a comprehensive introduction to sermon options and structures*. Grand Rapids, MI: Zondervan, 2006.

MacArthur, John, *Preaching*, Thomas Nelson, 2005

PIETERSE,H.J.G., 'Sermon Forms', Journal of Theology for Southern Africa, pp 10-17

Pollard, A., *English sermons, British council and National book league,* 1963, pp 37-43;

Tow Timothy, *My Homiletic Swimming Pool*, Far Eastern Bible College Press, Singapore, 1998

William H. Willimon, *A Guide to Preaching and Leading Worship,* Westminster Press, 1984

The article at the next pages was initially submitted by the author to the Theological Journal via the University of Birmingham but has been insert into this Introduction of the Art preaching course handbook to arouse those of having academic hanger who would want to amount to the degree level of theological programme. It may serve as a sample of a research document that often is required to be submitted in most of advanced academic programme. The contents of the article are relevant to this book.

THE EFFECTS OF POSTMODERNITY ON TODAY'S EVANGELISM AND THEIR IMPACT UPON CONTEMPORARY CHRISTIAN FAITH,

by Pastor Simon Nzubahimana, BA, PgDip,LLB, Pastor and Teacher at the World Outreach Church, Leicester, England.

The comparison of today's way of communicating the Christian message in the western society with the times of John Wesley and of the Welsh Revival may lead a postmodern evangelist to readjust the methodologies of outreaching today's audience. The academic world has found a best way to define today's audience's attitude as postmodernity.

The term *'postmodernity'* is mainly known in the academic milieu referring to the society's aspect of changes that is occurring in almost every day's lifestyle. Such apparent changes had compelled some missiologists such as Andrew Walls and Lamin Sannch[1]

---

1   Vanhoozer J.K., the Cambridge companion to postmodern theology, p.22

to wonder whether nowadays the Christian's mission would not need to be readjusted with the new realities of the postmodernity. The main question would be to know to which extend such readjustments may end up mainly after reading from Ghisi's analysis where he says that though today's society is leaning to "the [(1)] openness to spiritual guidance, it is [also (2)] moving away from vertical authority towards more "horizontal" organisations[2] ".

Yet despite the above signs of moving away from vertical authority spotlighted by Ghisi, the new recent spiritual big screen movies, such as The Passion of Christ and Da Vinci Code, that have proved to attract a big number of viewers in cinema halls and private houses, may lead one to assume that the postmodern society is more receptive to evangelism than its previous counterpart.

In his article 'What can the Church learn from the pied piper of postmodernity' David Couchman for instance says that "the Da Vinci Code has become a major cultural icon of our times".

---

2   Ghisi, Luyckz M. 'The Transmodern Hypothesis: Towards a Dialogue of Cultures', Futures, p.3

One of the Da Vinci Code's selling points is to "resonate with some central aspects of contemporary culture[3]"; the Christian mission may then reach the postmodern audience by recognising their current perceptive methods.

The problem would only be however, as Paul points it out in his letter to the Romans, on how they would follow Jesus whom they have not heard or whom they have not been appropriately told yet (Romans 10:14).

As no one would doubt about the dynamic change of today's society, the major question is to know how today's Christian mission can reach such society and examining the impact the current changes might have, if any, on the Christian faith.

The Church of Christ has always had an outreaching mission through various means including preaching and other ministries and should carry it on focussing mainly on reaching out youth in order to create Christian message's continuity between generations.

---

3   Couchman, David 'What can the Church learn from the pied piper of Postmodernity?' Evangel; Autumn2006, Vol. 24 Issue 3, p71-75

In order to keep such link between generations that have different perspectives due to those aspects of changes, it may be necessary to understand what postmodernity focuses on in regard to the Biblical truths. Commonly, the postmodernity's main weapon is to attack theory and methodology of the biblical stories of God's self-revelation to the world because of the impossibility to prove them on a rational and objective method that enables everyone to construct from the bottom up universal knowledge.

George Barna quoted by Tim Stafford and Greg Schneider in their article 'The third coming of George Barna' published in Christianity Today 46 no 9 Ag 5 2002, p 32-38, seems to say that only a small number (4%) of the general population have a biblical worldview and suggests that many of the nation's moral and spiritual challenges are directly attributable to this fact.

Reading the above comments from George Barna, one may understand that ignorance of the Biblical worldview is one of the main factors for moral and spiritual changes.

Yet the challenges are also linked with the fact that postmodern ideology rejects the authority of reason and views all claims to objective truth to be dangerous.

In the course of finding a compromising solution, Evangelical Christians are led to embrace some elements of the understanding of postmodernity and operate within the above define context which obviously may overstretch them in order to deal effectively with it.

The challenge is how they (Evangelical Christians) would conduct the Christian mission in such context.

This new context of embracing new changes puts the Christian's mission under intense pressure for it might need some readjustments to fit into the new realities of the postmodernity.

It may not be as a smooth transition as it may look due to the fact that postmodern society's perspectives, as quoted earlier by Ghisi, seems to have shifted away from the vertical authority.

Recently Ravi Zacharias was posing some more new questions in his book 'Jesus Among Other Gods' asking on

"How do you communicate with a generation that hears with its eyes and thinks with its feelings?[4]". In other words, he seemed to say that the postmodern society might have a different way of assessing things. It could also be one of the reasons the Emerging Church[5], is inviting churches to reshape their beliefs and practices to conform to postmodernism in order to be efficient in their outreaching the postmodern society.

However reshaping Christian beliefs and practices that have been in place for nearly 2000 years is not as easy as somebody would think.

As Willimon points it out, "the great evangelistic challenge is not to attract the world to the gospel but rather for an accommodated, acculturated church to be attracted to the world in the same strange way that Christ is attracted[6] ".

4   Dr Ravi Zacharias is also referred to by Dr Erwin W.Lutzer in his book, *Who are you Judge?, Learning to Distinguish between Truths, Halth-Truths and Lies*, page 24

5   According to Pettegrew, L.D, in his article 'Evangelicanism, paradigms and the Emerging Church' that recently appeared in Master's Seminary Journal 17 no 2 Fall 2006, p 159-175, A church that has appeared in attempt to minister to the postmodern culture.

6   Willimon H, 'Evangelism in the twenty-first century: mainliners

If such accommodating culture changes is a way forward, it would remain challenging to know to which extend someone would go to be culturally relevant to people, for there are some Scriptures' boundaries that require the Christian Church to "don't conform to the pattern of the world" (Romans 12:1- 2) while trying to reach it.

In such outreaching, it would be then better to double check to whether all outreach paths are leading to the same destination, otherwise Christianity's claim to be the only way to salvation would be baseless (Jn14:1).

In all attempts to outreach today's society, a better balance has to be found for according to Don Carson[7], and he might be right, "evangelism today must start with God, creation, and the fall. If we don't agree on the problem Jesus addressed, the solution won't be comprehensible".

Today's preachers may then require extra miles to outreaching 21st century type of society. Allen, Ronald J, believes that

at the margins' Journal for Preachers 30 no 4 Pentecost 2007, p 3-10
7   Carson, D.A., The Gagging of God: Christianity Confronts Pluralism. p. 573.

"the postmodern preacher, should recognise that every act of awareness is interpretive and help the community sorting out: (a) aspects of the emerging postmodern world that support their understanding of the gospel and Christian witness, (b) ways in which the gospel challenges postmodernism, and (c) dimensions of postmodernism that urge them to rethink parts of its notion of the gospel and Christian life[8]" .

In such circumstance, Richard Jensen, in his book 'Telling the Story: Variety and Imagination in Preaching', proposes that "preachers should move from didactic preaching to proclaimatory preaching and narrative preaching[9] ". Such move is also supported by Jolyon Mitchell quoting David Norrington saying that "preachers today should be aware of cultural limitation of their audience[10] " and suggests that traditional forms of preaching have no future and argue that preachers must find new forms which involve the

8   Allen, Ronald J.,' Preaching and postmodernism', Interpretation 55 no 1 January 2001, p 34-48.
9   Jensen, R.A Thinking in Story: Preaching in a Post-literate Age, p..
10   McKinnon, Gillian, 'Visually speaking: radio and the renaissance of preaching', Studies in World Christianity 6 no 2 2000, p 298-299.

congregation in participatory communication such as finding ways to listen to the congregation and to bring their perceptions into the sermon.

Listening to all the new outreaching theories, one may look confused for they seem to be no clear cut or directives to follow that would work most for everyone.

Byassee Jason in his article 'Emerging model: a visit to Jacob's Well' recalls a visit he made to Jacob's Well church where he found the worship to be far different from the other existing evangelical churches, where the congregation was more interactive.

According to him, "their songs were new, and the words were flashed up on a plasma screen by PowerPoint, though the language was as old as scripture[11] ".

He seems to propose that an interractive preaching model may be a part of the solutions. This interactive church model seems to be also supported by even Andy Crouch of Christianity Today,

11   Byassee, Jason, 'Emerging model: a visit to Jacob's Well' Christian Century 123 no 19 S 19 2006, p 21

though he was known to be often critical of much of the Emergent movement, he praises Jacob Well to be excellent for, as far as he can remember, it is "the best singing white church he has ever been to[12] ."

If such interactive church model would be more lively and helping preachers to reach today's society why can't it be reassessed and if necessary be adopted where it can work?

Otherwise if the proposed interactive Church is 'the Bible study style' sermon type, one may wonder whether the orderly public meeting of 1 Corinthians 14 outlining on how public worship ought to be with the goal of edifying the saints can still applying to the above type of postmodern congregation.

Though the postmodern society has its own way of perceiving the world, they should also have some minimum of common methods of worship that may lead an unbeliever attending newly a postmodern service to know Jesus Christ as his Lord and Saviour.

---

[12] Ibid., p.21

The other context one may like to assess is how postmodern youth may be evangelised. For if it is assumed that postmodern youth is much influenced by what is called 'electronic culture' such as movies, television, internet, or in other words, virtual reality which may be a hindrance for them to know "what is reality", it should also be an appropriate method that is suitable to convey them the Christian Gospel. Otherwise keeping on ignoring apparent reality of changes,young people may learn wrong message from wrong medium and end up with a different Gospel message.

In such circumstance, there could be a new generation of Christian Gospel which would be totally separated from the one handed down throughout generations.

If it is believed that postmodern youth's role models are often picked up from some of the celebrities' characters in the way they dress up, speak or behave, evangelising such group may require a process of building up relationships, meeting needs, bringing them into communities and many other strategies. That is probably what Dr John Sentamu, the Archbishop of York, was trying to achieve when he was attending a youth convention wearing a hoodie in Bradford 13 .

For, in doing so, he thought illustrating the prejudice young people often face on Britain's streets by wearing hoodies would identify him much with his audience and find an appropriate method to reach them. He began such approach based on the statistics he had (Dr. Sentamu) that "99% of those wearing hoodies are law-abiding citizens and [yet] in a rapidly changing culture, many are bewildered about how to communicate with young people". He probably seemed to demonstrate that in a postmodern society the Gospel should become flesh and dwell among the community in order to become more receptive, (Jn 1:14).

He also seems to say that the core component of the new approach is to engage a dialogue with youth.

However though he might have been able to make his point right, outreaching the postmodern society might be more than outfitting for as Don Carson puts it in 'The Gagging of God', "The good

13   12 BBC News 24, on 2nd of May 2006 (see http://news.bbc.co.uk/1/hi/england/bradford/4962624.stm)

news of Jesus Christ is virtually incoherent unless it is securely set into a biblical worldview14 ."

In the same way, Byassee, Jason15 challenges the readers that "the work of Jesus was not a new set of ideals or principles for reforming or even revolutionizing society, but the establishment of a new community, a people that embodied forgiveness, sharing and self-sacrificing love in its rituals and discipline".

Though reaching the youth presents a quiet number of challenges, one can still build up a more loving community, in which youth finds role model and experience the love of God in the love of others and in which they understand what it means to be the Body of Christ.

From what has just been said, no one denies that the postmodern society has shifted away from its existing lifestyle due to various reasons.

---

14   Carson, D.A., The Gagging of God: Christianity Confronts Pluralism. P. 573.
15   Byassee, J, op.cit. p 20-24

No one can deny either that their changes are not affecting the way the Christian message is being conveyed to them. Several philosophies and techniques are being tested and some of them may be useful, subject to their contexts.

The overall question is to know if there is any global medicine available that can be prescribed to all situations of the society.

In other words, the overall strategies would be also better to consider to whether the Christian message is conforming to what originated from the original message instead of attracting the world to Jesus with some sort of gospel that entices everyone and offends nobody.

And the final question is to know if the Church is targeting to convert the world or the world is targeting to convert the Church.

REFERENCES:

Allen, Diogenes. "Christian values in a post-Christian context." In Postmodern theology: Christian faith in a pluralist world, ed. Frederic B Burnham. 20-36. San Francisco: Harper & Row, 1989

Allen, Ronald J.,' Preaching and postmodernism', Interpretation 55 no 1 January 2001, p 34-48

BBC News 24, on 2nd of May 2006 (see http://news.bbc.co.uk/1/hi/england/bradford/4962624.stm)

Byassee, Jason 'Emerging model: a visit to Jacob's Well' Christian Century 123 no 19 S 19 2006, p 20-24

Carson, D A, ed. Telling the truth: Evangelizing postmoderns. Grand Rapids: Zondervan, 2000.

Carson, D.A., The Gagging of God: Christianity Confronts Pluralism. Grand Rapids: Zondervan Publishing House, 1996.

Couchman, David 'What can the Church learn from the pied piper of Postmodernity?' Evangel; Autumn 2006, Vol. 24 Issue 3, p71-75

References:

Dockery, David S, ed. The challenge of postmodernism: An evangelical engagement. Grand Rapids: Baker, 1997.

Gibbs, Eddie and Ian Coffey. Church next: Quantum changes in Christian ministry. Leicester, UK: Inter-Varsity Press, 2000.

Gibbs, Eddie and Ryan Bolger. 'Tracking the emerging church'. Journal of the American Society for Church Growth 15 (Winter 2004): 3-10.

Grenz, Stanley J. A primer on postmodernism. Grand Rapids: Eerdmans, 1996.

Jamieson, Alan. A churchless faith: Faith journeys beyond evangelical, Pentecostal and charismatic churches. Wellington, NZ: Philip Garside, 2000. Jensen R.A., Thinking in Story: Preaching in a Post-literate Age, Lima, OH: C. S. S. Publishing Co., 1993.

Johnson, Philip. 'Postmodernity, New Age, and Christian mission'. Lutheran Theological Journal 31 (1997): 115-124.

Jones, Tony. Postmodern Youth Ministry. Grand Rapids: Zondervan, 2001

McKinnon, Gillian, 'Visually speaking: radio and the renaissance of preaching', Studies in World Christianity 6 no 2 2000, p 298-299.

Mitchell,J.P., Visually Speaking: Radio and the Renaissance of Preaching, Edinburgh: Westminster John Knox Press, 2000

Stafford, Tim; Schneider, Greg in his article The third coming of George Barna published in Christianity Today 46 no 9 Ag 5 2002, p 32-38.

Vanhoozer J.K., The Cambridge Companion to Postmodern Theology, Cambridge: Cambridge University press, 2003.

Willimon, William H., Journal for Preachers 30 no 4 Pentecost 2007, p 3-10. Zacharias, R.J., Jesus Among Other Gods, USA:Nelson (Thomas) Publishers, 2001.

FINAL THOUGHT

This Practical Introduction To the Art of Preaching manual has been put together from the combined lecturer notes during the Teaching sessions of the Pastors and perspectives pastors in the City of Leicester.

In putting them together the Lecturer would like to make them available to any serving lay preacher who never had opportunity to be in a formal Bible College or any novice who would embark into the preaching ministry.

The book includes the Historical background of the ministry of preaching, the root cause of the preaching mandate, what an audience would expect from a standard sermon, some useful considerations when a preacher is invited to preach, different sermons structures and various types of sermons and some useful guidelines to deliver a standard sermon. It has also included various thoughts in the academic milieu about the postmodern audience. I hope they will of great help.

Please do not hesitate to contact me anytime you would have some other useful suggestions

www.ingramcontent.com/pod-product-compliance
Lightning Source LLC
Chambersburg PA
CBHW060651030426
42337CB00017B/2561